THE HOUSES OF RICHARD B. ISENHOUR

THE HOUSES OF RICHARD B. ISENHOUR

MID-CENTURY MODERN IN KENTUCKY

R. L. Isenhour

R. L. ISENHOUR

ISBN 978-1-935497-90-5

Library of Congress Control Number: 2014939776

Book design by Raymond L. Isenhour, Green Scheme Design LLC

Printed in Canada

Published by Butler Books
P.O. Box 7311
Louisville, Kentucky 40257
phone: (502) 897-9393
fax: (502) 897-9797

To order copies of this book visit online
www.butlerbooks.com

BUTLER BOOKS

PHOTOGRAPH CREDITS

page photographs

front cover	048 JARVIS	Photo: R. B. Isenhour 1960
back cover		
up left	046 ZECHELLA	Photo: R. L. Isenhour
up right	073 ELWOOD	Photo: R. L. Isenhour
lower	147 ISENHOUR	Photo: R. B. Isenhour 1972
page 2	048 JARVIS	Photo: R. B. Isenhour 1960
page 4	038 DUMMIT	Photo: R. B. Isenhour 1959
page 5	026 ISENHOUR	Photo: R. B. Isenhour 1957
page 6	034 PEDERSON	Photo: R. B. Isenhour 1958
page 10	041 SCHUETTE	Photo: R. B. Isenhour 1959
page 160	147 ISENHOUR	Photo: R. B. Isenhour 1972

Photographs used with permission:

page 15	147 KROGDAHL	© W. S. Krogdahl
pages 38–39	044 SCHWERT	© Photos by Gregory Luhan, AIA
pages 43–45	046 ZECHELLA	© Photos by Steven M. White, RA, LEED AP

Photographs by Richard B. Isenhour are noted along with
approximate year photo was taken. All drawings and sketches
are scans of original plans from the Richard B. Isenhour archives.

Unless noted otherwise all photographs
Copyright © 2014 by Raymond L. Isenhour

CONTENTS

R. B. ISENHOUR
DRAWING A CONTEMPORARY LINE

GRAHAM POHL

I have admired the works of architect and builder Richard B. Isenhour for as long as I've lived in Lexington. His houses are simple forms with clean lines. Limestone often alternates with wood paneled walls, and window openings are generous spans of glass that help organize the composition, marking transitions from one simple planar shape to another.

When I spoke with him, Richard Isenhour had retired from architecture and building, but he had created a remarkable legacy. I was fortunate to sit with him, his wife, and son to discover how he accomplished so much.

Isenhour's best work is full of light, creating an inspirational sense of the blending of outdoors and indoors. In many of his houses, walls are more than just part of the box that makes a space—they are articulated as planes that are independent of one another. For example, a wall of native limestone or wood paneling might be met by a plane of glass with minimal detail at the intersection, so that the wall seems to slide continuously through space, defining living zones while blurring separation between inside and outside. As we experience the house from the interior, such details subtly suggest that our personal experience of space can expand to infinity. From the exterior, Isenhour's sophisticated use of building materials clarifies these ideas and results in fresh and satisfying compositions.

The notion of personal space becoming infinite space is a Modernist idea, perhaps most elegantly expressed by Ludwig Mies van der Rohe at the Barcelona Pavilion in 1924. While similar ideas are evident in many of Isenhour's houses, the architect was never a spokesman for any particular architectural bent. His drawings were not aggressive statements—there was never any intent to draw a line in the architectural sand. Nor was he enchanted by the stars of architectural history. Rather, he was a man with remarkable powers of observation and a steadfast interest in making his own way, who, by looking and by building, came to discover some powerful strategies for making houses. His skills are perhaps most evident in the house he built for himself in 1972 at 2064 Bridgeport Drive.

Born in 1924, Richard Isenhour grew up in Charlotte, North Carolina. He studied chemical engineering in Raleigh and married Lenora Henry in 1947. She was the daughter of A. R. Henry, who developed Arcadia Park, Glendover, and Jesselin Drives in Lexington. Richard went to work for DuPont when he graduated, moving with Lenora to Newburgh, New York, for three years and then to their construction division in Kinston, North Carolina, for one year. He left DuPont because the corporate environment didn't suit him and because it appeared that the couple would have to move every few years. In 1952

044 SCHWERT 3316 Braemer Drive, Lexington Kentucky 1959

8   he started building houses with the help of his father-in-law. "I came to Lexington to learn how to build," he said. "I didn't work with him (A. R. Henry) because I wanted to work for myself... but I asked him a whole bunch of questions!" In 1958 Isenhour started studying architecture part time, graduating from the University of Kentucky ten years later. He became a registered architect in 1974.

The Isenhours had four children, all of whom stayed in or near Lexington, and nine grandchildren. The extended family was clearly an important part of the Isenhours' life, and Richard encouraged enough interest in the profession among his offspring and their spouses to result in two architecture degrees. One son, Paul, continues the home building tradition with Isenhour, Inc.

Richard Isenhour's houses were featured regularly in newspaper articles. Bettye Lee Mastin, retired *Lexington Herald-Leader* columnist, wrote articles on three of the Isenhours' personal homes—in 1954, 1961, and 1986. She covered other Isenhour houses in 1963, 1968, and 1980.

Where did Richard Isenhour find the courage and resolve to get this work built? I believe his ability to execute so many outstanding—and outstandingly different—houses came in part from the era in which he began to build. The '50s was a decade of optimism and growth. In the postwar years, renewed faith in technology and fresh pride in our culture encouraged exploration. Newness was celebrated, and the design world blossomed. Isenhour's first house, 328 Albany Road, was built in 1952. In 1953 he built a house for his own family at 213 Jesselin Drive. Although strong in their own rights these early houses don't reflect the style that was to typify his homes for the next three decades, but Isenhour was learning the trade and forming his own ideas in a culture that encouraged exploration.

Émigrés from Europe, including refugees from Hitler's elimination of the Bauhaus, had been building and designing in America since the late '30s, and by the '50s their work was well known and respected in architectural circles. Walter Gropius and Mies van der Rohe were particularly influential through their American architectural practices and teaching careers.

Richard Isenhour didn't credit Gropius or Mies for his vision (and he was too self-effacing to admit to being visionary). He attributed his inspiration to images in magazines and to travel. With his wife Lenora, Isenhour visited California in the mid '50s, bringing back reams of photos. They visited Europe with Sir Banister Fletcher's *A History of Architecture* in hand. They saw mitered corner windows with no corner column in contemporary homes in Mexico. They visited Philip Johnson's glass house

147 ISENHOUR 2064 Bridgeport Drive, Lexington, Kentucky 1972

in New Canaan, Connecticut, and Frank Lloyd Wright's houses in Oak Park, Illinois, Fallingwater in Pennsylvania, and Taliesin West in Arizona.

It was clear during our discussion that Richard Isenhour always had more than a passing interest in architecture— even long before he formalized his architectural studies at the University of Kentucky. In the years before he started building houses, when the Isenhours lived in New York and North Carolina, the couple exploited opportunities presented by their new locations. They brought open minds and healthy curiosities, and they toured and learned.

Lenora had strong feelings about how a modern family wants to live in a house, and she encouraged her husband to develop the signature open floor plan used in their own home. Together they moved beyond the traditional world so well represented in Lexington. That they adopted a contemporary open plan was unusual enough in Lexington. That Isenhour built crisply contemporary houses expressing the new under-standing was truly remarkable.

Richard Isenhour started building open floor plan houses over 60 years ago. In some ways the market has caught up with him today. Many houses on the market now feature open floor plans—they work well for how we live and they encourage a sense of generous space, even in economical packages. What almost all of these new houses lack is a form that recognizes the leap from the classical closed floor plan to the contemporary open idea. They suffer from the schizophrenic attempt to look traditional on the outside while offering contemporary living on the inside. What differentiates Isenhour's work from much of what is sold today is that he created a building form that honestly and powerfully expressed the open plan and that fully exploited the spatial opportunities presented by the plan.

Having been fortunate enough to spend some time with the Isenhours I can assure you that one of the reasons Richard Isenhour was so successful is that he followed his muse without worrying too much about what others thought and that he did this with great heart. Lenora (who for 22 years was the executive director of the predecessor to First Link, a volunteer services organization) wrote, "A house is a 'home' only as long as you live there. When you take your family and all your 'stuff,' that home becomes a house again. Wherever the people you love reside—that's home."

Sentiment was evident in the Isenhour home, and, without a doubt, the contemporary line glows a little brighter when it's drawn by a loving hand.

INTRODUCTION

Today the term "mid-century modern" designates a design movement in American housing that began after World War II and lasted into the 1970s. Families had doubled up during the Depression and were ready to spread out. Millions of returning veterans benefitted from a new G. I. bill that included education grants and mortgage loan guarantees. The postwar era was a time of new beginnings, with young families demanding new houses. During this period, some architects and homebuilders started to create a new look for the modern age.

Lexington, Kentucky, architect Richard B. Isenhour did not know the term mid-century modern nor did he later use it to describe his designs. Along with architects across the nation, Isenhour focused on new design goals—simple lines, open living areas, connection to the outdoors, and use of natural materials. However, he never voiced a feeling of being or wanting to be part of any movement. He felt he was one person working in a small town, finding his way by turning over one stone at a time.

Isenhour's designs and design philosophy came out of looking at his surroundings and paying close attention to what he saw. During family vacations, his children often grew impatient when he stopped at a realtor's office and asked where the local "contemporary" houses were located. He proceeded to drive by those houses and was even known to walk into people's yards to take photos, much to the chagrin of his wife, Lenora. He leafed through housing magazines like *House Beautiful* and later architectural magazines, cutting or ripping out pictures of details and ideas he liked and organizing them in folders.

Fayette County lies in the heart of Kentucky. Between 1950 and 1980, its population more than doubled, increasing from 100,746 to 204,165. Whole subdivisions sprang up, many on the south side of Lexington where the typical new home might be a one-story brick with double-hung windows and shutters. Larger houses might be two-story southern colonial with steep roof pitches and porches with columns.

Some of the rapid expansion was due to IBM opening a new facility and the University of Kentucky building the Chandler Medical Center and creating the College of Medicine. Both projects brought new families to Lexington, many from other regions of the country where different designs were appearing. Some of these newcomers were drawn to Isenhour's houses, which were at the time unusual for Lexington.

By the 1960s there was a public awareness of the contemporary look of Lexington's new houses, and they started to be known as "Isenhour houses." To the owners and admirers, it was a point of pride, but for others it may not have been offered as a compliment.

Richard and Lenora Isenhour moved to Lexington 1952

002   *328 Albany Road, Lexington, Kentucky 1952*

12   Richard Isenhour was born in 1924 and grew up in Charlotte, North Carolina. His father was an administrator for AT&T. The construction influence may have come from his grandfather, Jacob Monroe Isenhour, who was a carpenter constructing homes north of Charlotte, including his own house at Claremont. Growing up, Richard Isenhour had a talent for sketching and cartooning but did not seriously consider these as career options.

He joined the V-12 Navy College Training Program and spent time on the campuses of the University of Virginia in Charlottesville, Columbia University in New York City, and Northwestern University in Chicago. He was commissioned as an ensign at Northwestern. After the war he attended North Carolina State University where he completed a degree in chemical engineering. He took his first job with DuPont in Newburgh, New York, in 1947 and soon married Lenora Henry from Lexington, Kentucky.

In an early letter to Lenora Henry, Isenhour questioned his career choice: "The kind of job I'd like would be one that's creative and always changing, where I can see what I'm accomplishing. I'd like to work on things I can improve...sometimes I think I missed my calling." In 1951 he transferred from a manufacturing plant to the construction division of DuPont in Kinston, North Carolina. After four years with a large company, he knew

he wanted to work for himself, and in 1952 the Isenhours moved to Lenora Henry's hometown to start a new career.

Like the clients who would purchase Isenhour's houses, the couple was raised during the Depression and came of age during World War II. They appreciated the need for housing that was modest and functional, but they were also future-oriented, sharing in the postwar optimism of their generation. Lexington was the perfect market, appealing to those who anticipated a new style of living.

Isenhour's father-in-law A. R. Henry was a developer and house contractor in Lexington and a source of information as Richard Isenhour started his own company. Isenhour's first two complete houses, 328 Albany (see Job 002) and 195 Jesselin (see Job 004) built in 1952, used traditional details similar to other houses in the area. He worked on his own projects during the day, and then in the evening when workers were gone, he walked through A. R. Henry's houses to see how he handled certain details. A basic concept Isenhour learned was the importance of quality in construction. Throughout his contracting career, Isenhour stressed the importance of details being executed to such a high standard that few carpenters and subcontractors had the ability or patience to work on his projects.

004   195 Jesselin Drive, Lexington, Kentucky 1952

005   213 Jesselin Drive, Lexington, Kentucky 1953

In 1953 he built the house at 213 Jesselin (see Job 005) that the Isenhour family lived in for a while. The next several houses were built on Glendover Road. While they may not have looked noticeably different from other houses on the street, they began to reveal innovative ideas inside. In the living room and kitchen areas, Isenhour sloped the inside ceiling, attaching it to the underside of the roof rafters to create a cathedral ceiling. This technique gave more visual space to the rooms and made it easier to tie living areas together. To make the interior space work, the roof pitch had to become lower, which also reduced the roof as a major visual element. At 222 Glendover (see Job 019) and 322 Glendover (see Job 021) built in 1954, the side elevations have high gable windows opening to show the cathedral ceiling space inside.

Although he had limited experience with what was happening in design, Isenhour had some important early influences on his work. In the summer of 1955, Richard and Lenora Isenhour took a three-week car tour to the west coast. Here he drove through San Francisco neighborhoods and saw firsthand some of the new ideas being incorporated into dwellings of the postwar period. Joseph Eichler had started building houses in the Palo Alto area in 1949 and 1950, where he brought a new modernism to the postwar suburbs.

019   222 Glendover Road, Lexington, Kentucky 1954

021   322 Glendover Road, Lexington, Kentucky 1954

House north of San Francisco, California 1955

House in Morro Bay, California 1955

14

Other developers were influenced by these houses, and a California-modern style with open glass areas began to appear. The labels on the slides taken on the Isenhour trip included Kentfield and Belvedere, areas north of San Francisco in Marin County. The first Eichler development in this area was Terra Linda in San Rafael, begun in 1955. While it does not appear that Isenhour saw any Eichler homes on this trip, he was able to see other houses built in the "bring-the-outside-in" style Eichler advertised. Isenhour's photo of two unknown houses (see photos above) shows the post-and-beam construction typical of some of these houses, which certainly influenced his work when he returned to Lexington.

His interest in post-and-beam construction versus traditional wall construction was revolutionary for Lexington. Wall construction implied that the walls of a house would be built from two-by-fours, with openings for windows and doors "punched" into the exterior walls. Post-and-beam construction gave a different visual result. A post-and-beam system still relies on a system of walls to help separate inside from outside and room from room. The difference is that these walls are not structural, so they can be built of any height and of any material. Windows became expanses of glass. Post-and-beam construction lent itself to modern open floor plans and contemporary design.

Post-and-beam construction was only one of several focuses previously unseen in Lexington, but which Isenhour shared with other designers. He also experimented with private front façades, cathedral ceilings, open floor plans and expanded living spaces, large areas of glass, atriums and patios, carports, innovative materials developed in wartime laboratories, and built-in cabinets that provided an uncluttered appearance.

The Isenhour construction crew was skilled in building one-of-a-kind custom homes usually designed solely by Isenhour; however, they sometimes built houses designed by other architects. In 1961 he worked with local architect John Morgan on the Krogdahl house (see Job 052). It has a flat roof, brick walls inside and out, and an attached carport. In 1962 he built the Nelson house (see Job 059) designed by the California architectural firm Campbell & Wong. Isenhour's attention to detail gave him the ability to take on this project. Door, window, and trim details specified for this house may have influenced how Isenhour understood choices for finish work. Later in 1970 the Scott house designed by Sam Halley and Joe Williams and in 1975 the Wheeler house designed by Don Wallace made him more aware of his own designs and details.

Isenhour's library included various books by and about Frank Lloyd Wright, including a worn and underlined copy of the

052 KROGDAHL   designed by John Morgan 1961

059 NELSON   designed by Campbell & Wong 1962

1954 book *The Natural House.* Noted was Wright's discussion of mixing new materials such as concrete, steel, and glass with old ones such as stone and wood in an "organic" new way. Isenhour's notes also focused on Wright's discussion of the Usonian house, with its "single spacious, harmonious unit of living room, dining room and kitchen."

The introduction to the bigger design world started around 1958 when Isenhour began taking design studio classes as a part-time student in the newly-formed College of Architecture at the University of Kentucky. There he studied with Charles Graves, Clyde Carpenter, and Don Wallace, among others. In 1968 he received a second bachelor's degree, this one in architecture.

When Richard Isenhour died in 2006, a *Lexington Herald-Leader* article described his work as "against the grain contemporary homes." Clyde Carpenter described Isenhour houses as "handsome examples of modern design," and Caruthers Coleman called them "simple structures, clearly expressed, and without a lot of garbage on them to try to imitate something else."

This collection documents many of the houses Isenhour designed and built between 1956 and 1978 in the most accurate way possible, using the plans, photos, and information from Richard Isenhour's own job files. These files include design notes from meetings with original clients and notes from the clients themselves. All drawings in this text are reproduced from his original pencil drawings on Clearprint, and all design sketches were drawn by Isenhour. Whenever possible, Isenhour's original negatives and slides are used and credited along with the approximate year the photo was taken. Information included in this book also comes from interviews with original clients and people he worked with as well as family members. Original owners or current owners were welcoming and enjoyed talking about their houses. The photos included in this collection try to show the houses as originally designed and built, including any additions later done by Isenhour.

When Isenhour retired in the late 1980s, company accounts showed 98 new building projects, including three commercial structures and 95 houses. (To date only one house has been torn down: Job 029, built in 1957 for Erwin on Clinton Road.) Twelve house designs were built by others or were never built.

The following pages document 43 early houses chronologically, showing the distinctive nature of Isenhour houses and how his designs evolved. Each house is identified by the original job number Isenhour assigned to the project and the name of the original owner.

1956
310 BLUEBERRY LANE
LEXINGTON KENTUCKY

026 ISENHOUR

By 1956, records show Richard Isenhour had designed and constructed 10 houses in the four years since he arrived in Lexington. Of these 10 houses, the Isenhour family had lived in two of them. When a buyer made an offer on a house, the family moved into the next house being built.

But by 1956 they were ready to settle down with their children and build a home they would live in for the next 16 years. While his designs had continued to evolve, Isenhour took a quantum leap with this 11th house, Job 026, the Isenhour house at 310 Blueberry Lane. It proved to be a key step to many distinctive designs that followed.

The trip to California the previous summer may have fueled the desire to make this house bolder. Freed up from designing for the expectations of a client, Isenhour could use this house as a design lab, a full-size model using fieldstone, redwood, and glass in a new way to bring in light and open up the plan. The lot had many trees, including elms, and Isenhour designed the house to fit around them. Stone was gathered from the Anderson County farm of his father-in-law, A. R. Henry. Sliding glass doors opened the house to a large screen porch.

The resulting design was a billboard that attracted additional clients. This house contains the seeds that continued to grow for 35 years.

19

Front Elev.

Rear Elev.

1957
314 BLUEBERRY LANE
LEXINGTON KENTUCKY

028 BULLARD

The Bullard house features the low sloping roofs that were a distinctive element of Isenhour's early houses. With the lower roof line, attics, dormers, and unneeded false heights disappear. Low slope allowed the overhanging eaves to extend farther. All of this increased the horizontal line of the roof and gave a distinctive "contemporary" look to the house.

The low slope has the additional advantage of allowing the interior ceiling to follow the underside of the roof rafters, making sloped cathedral ceilings possible. These higher, sloped ceilings are an important design element for interior space quality. For a given floor area, the space appears visually larger with higher ceilings, and it is possible to tie areas together with the higher visual space. Cathedral ceilings allow gable end areas above exterior walls to be filled with glass, thus admitting more light.

The post-and-beam construction evident in the rear walls of the house allows for an oversized sliding glass door.

This house bears a Bluegrass Trust Plaque, marking it as one of Lexington's "buildings of architectural or historical significance that are 50 or more years old." Many of Isenhour's earlier houses are also eligible for this distinction.

1957
697 BERRY LANE
LEXINGTON KENTUCKY

032 MILLS

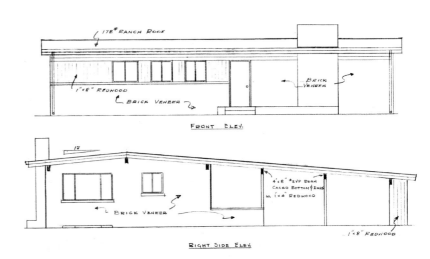

The use of windows continued to evolve in early Isenhour houses. In the Mills house, Isenhour includes punched window openings, which was typical for the time. However, these windows are aluminum, touted for requiring minimum maintenance—no rusting or need to repaint. Aluminum was one of the "new" materials, promising to revolutionize residential building.

The original design did not show a window to the right of the chimney, which would have created a partial solid masonry wall facing toward the street. This design look is shown in the artist's rendering on the right.

1957
341 BLUEBERRY LANE
LEXINGTON KENTUCKY

033 HITE

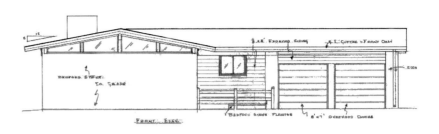

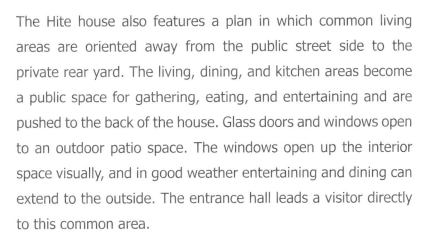

The Hite house also features a plan in which common living areas are oriented away from the public street side to the private rear yard. The living, dining, and kitchen areas become a public space for gathering, eating, and entertaining and are pushed to the back of the house. Glass doors and windows open to an outdoor patio space. The windows open up the interior space visually, and in good weather entertaining and dining can extend to the outside. The entrance hall leads a visitor directly to this common area.

The bedrooms and baths become a wing apart from the public areas. These rooms are private compartments away from the shared common space.

Without punched window openings, the front masonry wall becomes a solid rectangular design element, a bold choice in 1957. Light enters through the high clerestory windows above this wall, and the roof floats on posts above.

1958
342 BLUEBERRY LANE
LEXINGTON KENTUCKY

034 PEDERSON

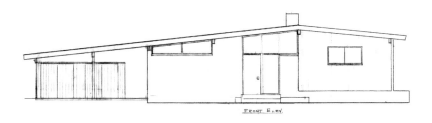

Photo: R. B. Isenhour 1958

As in many other Isenhour-designed houses, the Pederson house features interior walls between the living space, dining space, and kitchen that stop short of the ceiling. These non-load-bearing walls, sometimes called "pony walls," allow light to flow unblocked from room to room. Isenhour had used this detail in his own house just down the street. The owner of a similar house reported overhearing a stranger comment, "I wonder when they are going to finish their walls?" Like pony walls, the built-in cabinets partition spaces while preserving a sense of openness.

Isenhour departs from a traditional norm dictating that each room of a house should be enclosed by a door and given a name indicating its function. The raised ceiling above these walls makes the open plan read as one large space. In a house with a small footprint, the space seems larger visually and less claustrophobic.

Natural light flows into all spaces from the high triangular windows of the house, further uniting kitchen and living spaces. In what would become an oft-used element in his designs, Isenhour crafted the interior fireplace wall from the same stone used on the exterior. He extended the fireplace wall beyond the glass to meld the interior and exterior spaces and strengthen the sense that the patio was an outdoor extension of the house.

Photo: R. B. Isenhour 1958

28

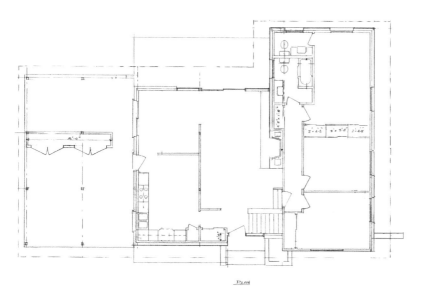

1958
3216 BRECKENWOOD DRIVE
LEXINGTON KENTUCKY

038 DUMMIT

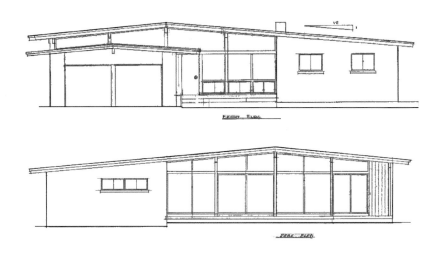

With no prospective clients in the fall of 1958, Isenhour purchased a lot from the Lansdowne Company and started to work on a design to build for sale. He selected a lot that would be rejected by any sensible contractor because it had mature trees growing in a swale right on the front building line. He overcame this challenge by pulling the garage forward and running the house behind the garage, as well as behind the trees, leaving them to work naturally with the design of the house. He also incorporates a limestone retaining wall that visually extends the façade of the house, making it appear taller.

Post-and-beam construction was a typical design method used in early Isenhour houses, and Isenhour fully exploits its advantages in this house. Beams run front to back through the house and visually extend out to the soffit and structurally carry the roof. Posts support beams, creating vertical elements that frame the glass. Posts eliminate the need of interior walls to support the roof, which opens up the space between living, dining, and kitchen. The posts allow the high windows that go across the front and the back of the house. The rear wall of the living area becomes all glass, side to side and top to bottom. Originally this total glass wall was recessed back from the rear wall leaving a screen porch across the back wall.

32

1959
349 JESSELIN DRIVE
LEXINGTON KENTUCKY

041 SCHUETTE

Front

In many early Isenhour house designs, the carport or garage becomes a design element. The car was an ever-increasing part of family life in the 1950s, and it moves from being sheltered in a detached outbuilding to being part of the house.

In the Schuette house, Isenhour places a solid brick wall that creates one wall of the carport and shields the house from the street. The wall stops short of the roof to let natural light into the kitchen windows behind. The roof over the carport is supported by posts and beams in the same design and scale that the interior roof is supported, and they both open to the outside.

1959
3316 BRAEMER DRIVE
LEXINGTON KENTUCKY

044 SCHWERT

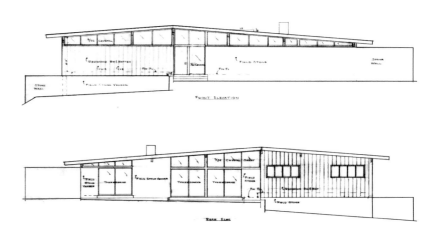

By the time Richard Isenhour began designing the Schwert house in 1959, he had grown adept at using a design vocabulary that made his houses easily recognizable. Here, Isenhour had the opportunity to use that vocabulary on a larger scale.

To the viewer seeing the Schwert house for the first time, the message is "this residence is private." Punched windows have been eliminated from the front elevation. Windows on the front are tucked just under the eaves, framed by the posts that carry the roof. The front wall consists of planes of native Kentucky stone and redwood siding, with battens used to cover the joints.

The Schwerts moved to Lexington in 1959 when Dr. Schwert became founding chair of the Department of Biochemistry in the College of Medicine, then being organized at the University of Kentucky. As was so often the case when his clients moved from other parts of the country, Isenhour found that they brought a different set of aspirations for what a house could be. This was particularly true for the group of doctors who came to Lexington at this time.

Isenhour later designed a studio addition to the house, by extending an upper section at the rear of the house. In 2007 April Pottorff, AIA, and Gregory Luhan, AIA, designed the renovation.

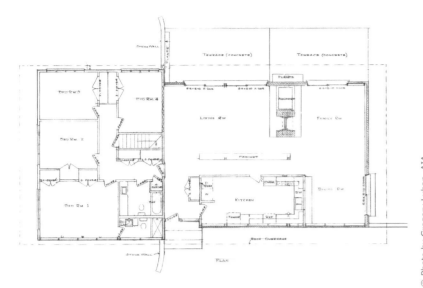

1959
3416 BELVOIR DRIVE
LEXINGTON KENTUCKY

045 TROUTMAN

FRONT ELEV.

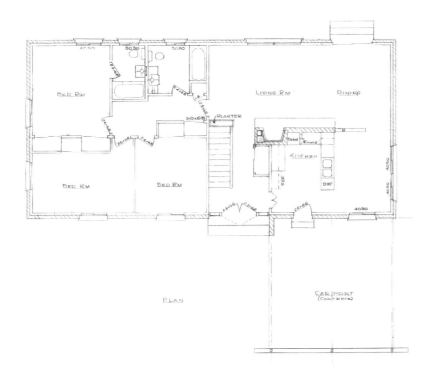

PLAN

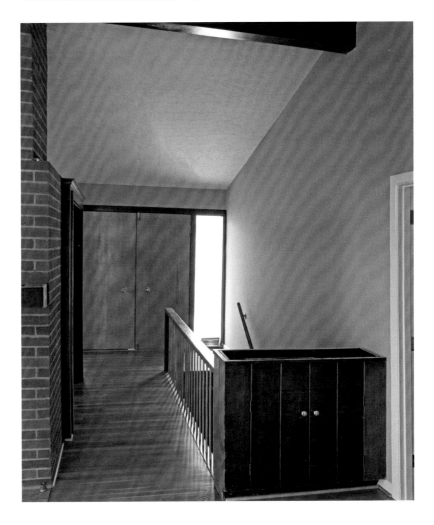

The Troutman house also features a carport, a popular mid-century design element. While America had firmly committed to its love affair with the car, architects like Frank Lloyd Wright preferred a carport to a garage. In *The Natural House,* Wright wrote that the garage could be eliminated. After all, a carport, with overhead protection and walls on two sides, provided adequate shelter for the modern car, built so that it no longer leaked. "Detroit still has the livery-stable mind," he wrote. "It believes that the car is a horse that must be stabled."

For Wright the open carport had the added advantage of exposing unnecessary clutter to public view, thereby discouraging its accumulation. Richard Isenhour shared Wright's dislike of clutter, and in fact, the idea of exchanging garage for carport is one of the underlined items in his copy of Wright's book. However, he sometimes provided his clients with a graceful solution by designing and building an enclosed storage area at carport's rear.

1960
345 JESSELIN DRIVE
LEXINGTON KENTUCKY

046 ZECHELLA

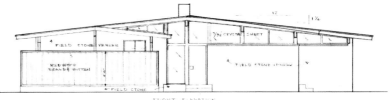

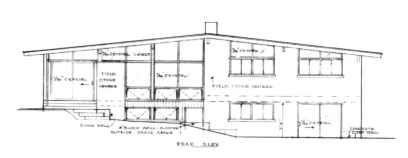

The Zechella house combines street appeal with what owners came to collectively call the "wow" moment: the experience of realizing that a particular Isenhour house would be the house for them. That moment often took place as the viewer walked through the front door and had a first look at open space and an expansive view through rear glass walls.

It's possible that the low rooflines and reasonable sizes of these early houses gave them the appearance of being among the smallest dwellings in the neighborhood. Expectations might have been kept low. That may have amplified the interior experience: the sense of spaciousness provided by high ceilings and the abundance of light provided by gable glass windows. Then other details kept heads turning: the stone wall and fireplace, the exposed redwood beams and trim, and wood floors.

All these elements make the houses inviting and livable. Even after a number of years, this feeling of a comfortable and relaxing living space is the most distinctive element tying all of Isenhour's houses together.

45

1960
342 JESSELIN DRIVE
LEXINGTON KENTUCKY

048 JARVIS

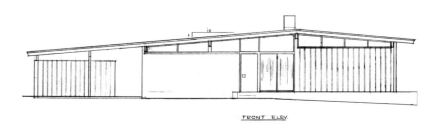

FRONT ELEV.

The Jarvis house shares elements with houses of the previous four years, but here the mathematical precision of the front elevation reflects a growing attention to details and proportion.

In this house, the dimensions of the brick wall left of the door and the dimensions of the wood wall to the right of the door are visually the same. The entrance area between brick and wood is half their width. The roof is designed so the windows above the wood wall mirror the windows above the brick. A similar vocabulary seen in earlier designs becomes more precise, cleaner. As a beginning student in the College of Architecture, Isenhour may have paid more attention to these details.

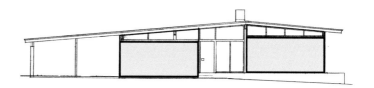

Shown during its construction phase, the Jarvis house is the full-page photo opposite the title page and as completed is the house shown on the cover of this book. This house was originally built for sale. The large number of surviving photos were probably taken for publicity purposes.

The center two workers in the 1960 construction photo are Bob Fox (second from left) and Leland Thompson (third from left), the original crew that was responsible for the exceptional quality work done on all of these early houses.

1961
337 JESSELIN DRIVE
LEXINGTON KENTUCKY

049 WINER

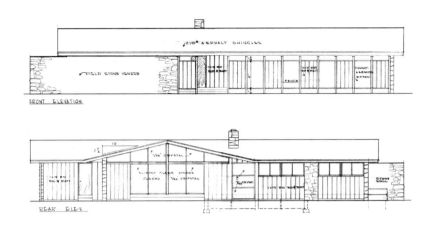

The majority of the early houses were custom built for a client with specific requirements. Clients typically came to Isenhour because they were drawn to the distinctive qualities of his other houses they had seen, but they wanted a design adapted for their unique situation.

Isenhour came up with the high double-gabled ceiling and glass across the back of the living space of this house in response to the client's request, itemized in his pre-design interview notes. These clients requested a living room large enough for entertaining and featuring lots of rear windows.

The modest and low-slung front façade, hidden from street view behind a fenced-in courtyard, belies the spaciousness and innovative design of this house's interior. This front courtyard is a design element that Isenhour would return to in later houses, even as he experimented with more modern forms. Courtyards, patios, and porches all helped houses of a modest size live larger than their square footage might imply.

1961
334 JESSELIN DRIVE
LEXINGTON KENTUCKY

051 MEAD

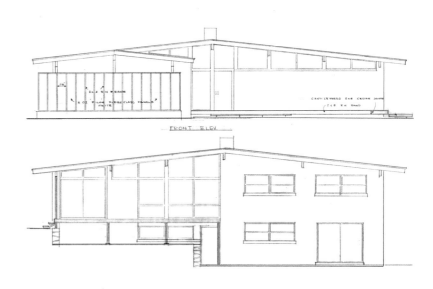

FRONT ELEV.

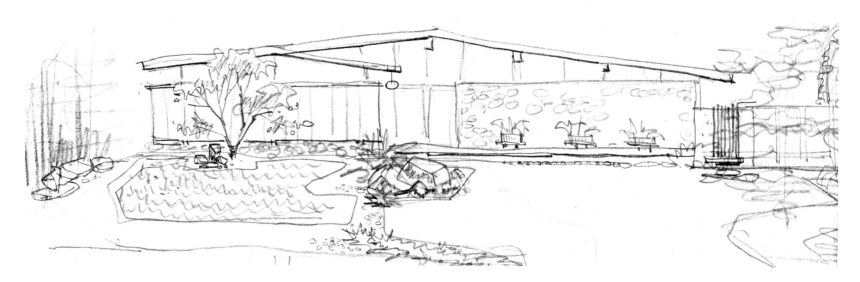

Richard Isenhour was known for specifying building materials suggestive of a natural environment. However, the post-World War II architect also had a variety of plastics available for various applications.

For the Mead house, a streetside screen was originally planned in redwood board and batten. However, sometime during the building process, Filon® panels were substituted for redwood boards. Filon is a fiberglass reinforced polyester that incorporates parallel nylon strands. While synthetic plastics were sometimes used to provide contrast between materials, it is more likely that the Filon panels were chosen for their translucent qualities, which would have allowed more light to enter the master bedroom area located just on the other side of the carport.

Filon was one of several synthetic plastics specified by mid-century designers, including laminates like Formica, acrylics like Plexiglass and Lucite, and vinyl upholstery options such as Fabrilite. Isenhour might have discovered Filon in Sweet's Catalog, a multi-volume publication that described building materials and their properties. However, his knowledge of modern mid-century products may have come from a more direct source. Lucite and Fabrilite, for example, were manufactured by Richard Isenhour's former employer, DuPont.

1961
4008 MAYFLOWER ROAD
LEXINGTON KENTUCKY

053 COHN

Over the next several years, Richard Isenhour received the opportunity to design and build houses in the Colony just off Versailles Road in Lexington. This subdivision, located farther from the city center, offered bigger lots. The developer had preserved the contours of the Bluegrass fields, formerly a part of the Sturgill property. The two-third acre lots with mature trees and more slope created site challenges and design opportunities; however, Isenhour chose to preserve trees whenever possible.

These commissions in the Colony also included larger houses, reflecting the greater prosperity of Lexington in the 1960s. With the expansion of the university and the development of clean industries like IBM, Lexington increased in population, and two-thirds of those new inhabitants came from out of state.

In many ways the Cohn House is a transition away from the California-style, post-and-beam, sloped-roof design that occupied Isenhour's interest for the first decade of his career. Perhaps as his architectural studies deepened, and he was exposed to the work of European architects who favored the International Style, he began to explore other possibilities. However, these explorations were always in conjunction with the local materials and design elements that reflected the developing Isenhour aesthetic.

1962
1265 COLONIAL DRIVE
LEXINGTON KENTUCKY

057 MENGUY

1963
1269 STANDISH WAY
LEXINGTON KENTUCKY

061 WEISS

In the Colony, Isenhour developed forms he further explored for houses in subdivisions that popped up around the city later in the decade. These houses were flat-roofed and two-storied and featured boxed volumes with wooden cubes set on top of stone. Covered spaces were created by overhanging upper levels.

These choices may reflect Isenhour's increasing exposure to the International Style in his design program at the College of Architecture. The direction of modern design was being influenced by Walter Gropius and Marcel Breuer who had left Germany at the outbreak of World War II and promoted the modernist ideas of the Bauhaus as professors at Harvard Graduate School of Design.

The Weiss House is a good example of some characteristics of the International Style. The house is composed of arranged volumes that are balanced rather than symmetrical. The International Style favored simple lines and pure forms. The same striving towards simplification, honesty, and clarity is identifiable in the works of other American architects in the 1960s.

Isenhour was able to work these principles in combination with his signature stone and redwood building materials. Houses in the Colony were often nestled in stands of mature trees, further solidifying Isenhour's respect for a Central Kentucky vocabulary.

Photo: R. B. Isenhour 1963

Photo: R. B. Isenhour 1963

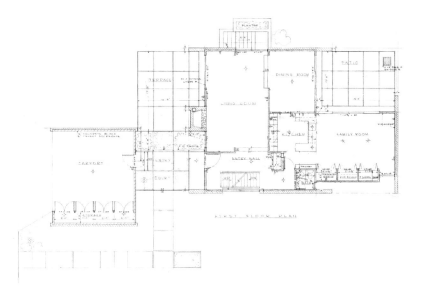

1964
341 JESSELIN DRIVE
LEXINGTON KENTUCKY

064 ROVIN

FRONT ELEVATION

The forms of the Rovin House are reminiscent of another International Style residence: the Philip Johnson Glass House in New Canaan, Connecticut. However, the Rovin House is sited in a residential neighborhood, rather than on a 37-acre campus, so providing privacy was important.

Here the volumes are screened by mature trees, and sliding screens cover glass doors that open to an outdoor porch and patio. The patio is shielded by vegetation.

When the current owner considered whether or not to purchase, she consulted her father. His advice was the following: "It's an Isenhour house. You have to get this house!"

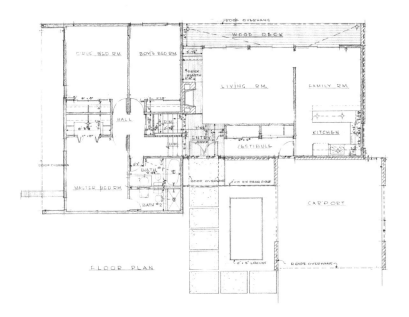

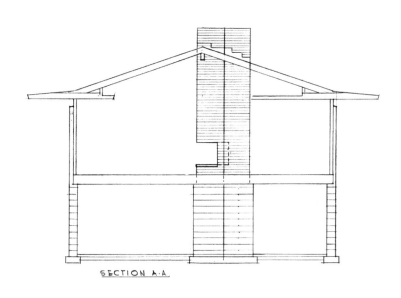

SECTION A·A

1964
635 NAKOMI DRIVE
LEXINGTON KENTUCKY

066 WESLEY

The design sketch was a useful way to present preliminary ideas to the owner. Sketches were often made on thin yellow tracing paper. Sometimes they were later marked up and used as a drawing board to discuss changes for the final plans. The preliminary sketch (above) shows a freestanding fireplace and continuous glass on the back and east side of the house that were in the design originally but not in the final construction plans.

The Wesley house features very large overhangs (five feet) that are structurally balanced on a beam to form a light shelf inside. This wood lintel band is continuous around the house, being visually carried by the stone, and it supports the horizontal soffit plane above. The section shows how the roof pitch was stopped at the wall line, making the horizontal cantilever and the roof less massive.

The Wesley house is a good example of a roof that extends out into the landscape to define and shelter an outdoor area. It also serves to regulate how sunlight will enter interior spaces.

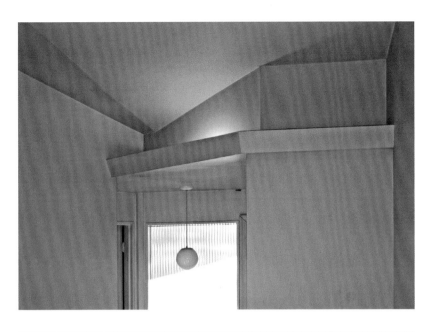

1964
3167 ROXBURG DRIVE
LEXINGTON KENTUCKY

067 GALLAHER

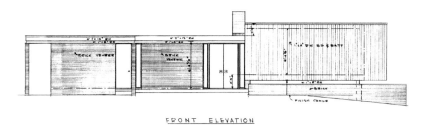

FRONT ELEVATION

"A house without shutters" was what Art and Dixie Gallaher specified when they moved to Lexington. They had lived in Oklahoma, Arizona, and Ireland and admired the work of contemporary architects like Bruce Goff.

Faced in brick rather than Isenhour's trademark local stone, the volumes of the Gallaher house also reveal a kinship with the International Style, which favored breaking a single mass into parts. These volumes group discrete functions: living, dining, and kitchen; bedrooms; and family room and study. While appearing private from the street, the house has 28 feet of glass overlooking the deep backyard.

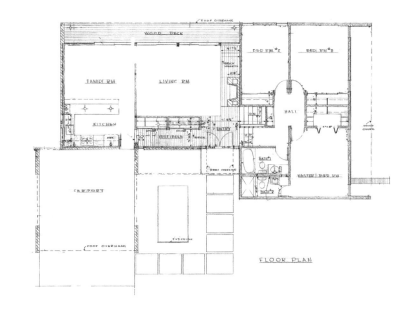

FLOOR PLAN

1964
806 OVERBROOK CIRCLE
LEXINGTON KENTUCKY

069 SURAWICZ

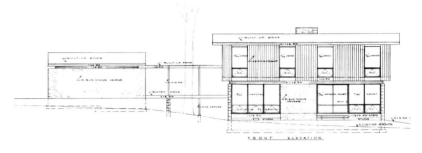

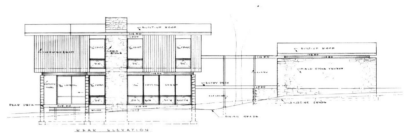

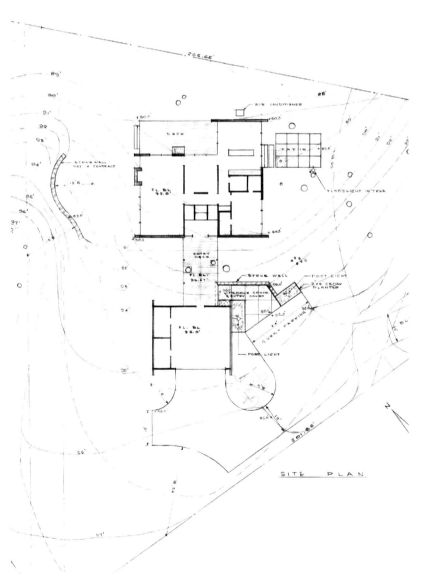

SITE PLAN

1965
755 BRAVINGTON WAY
LEXINGTON KENTUCKY

073 ELWOOD

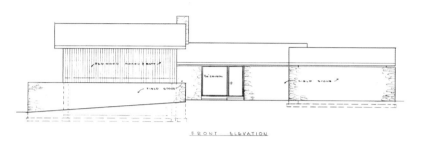

FRONT ELEVATION

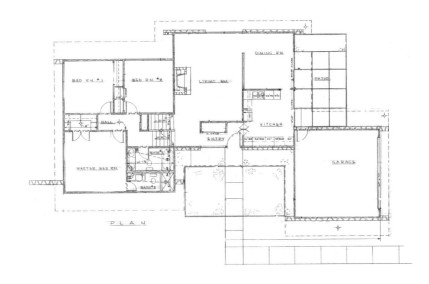

PLAN

1966
802 OVERBROOK CIRCLE
LEXINGTON KENTUCKY

078 WEIDNER

FRONT ELEVATION

The Weidners came to the University of Kentucky from the University of Hawaii. They contracted with Richard Isenhour to design a house and corresponded about the construction via air mail from Honolulu. The result is a large sheaf of letters that document construction progress, material choices, and change orders made during 1966.

This house continues to explore and refine favorite Isenhour themes. Glass walls bring the outside in and the inside out. A combination of glass doors and glass panes creates open walls, which connect the interior open area and outside private area. Glass doors make circulation to the outside possible in good weather for private living and entertaining. The high windows at both the front and back of the house let in light and extend the visual space. The ceiling and outdoor soffit are in the same plane, visually extending the interior ceiling outside. The interior stone wall aligns with the exterior stone wall which blurs the distinction between indoor space and outdoor space. Glass areas open to the rear yard and pool, a fitting transition for clients coming from the tropics. The front courtyard features an early sculpture by John R. Henry.

Later the University of Kentucky owned the house, and it was briefly the home for the family of one university president, who found the glass walls too extensive for their comfort.

90

1966
333 JESSELIN DRIVE
LEXINGTON KENTUCKY

079 MANDELSTAM

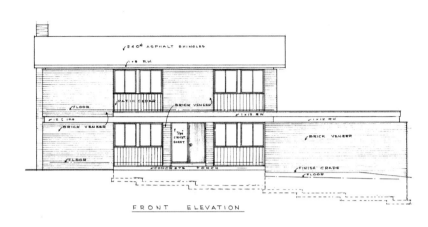

The Mandelstam house was the last of seven houses built at the east end of Jesselin Drive, five along the north side and two across on the south side of the street. This is the largest grouping of Isenhour houses, and they illustrate the design changes that occurred in the seven years from 1959 to 1966. Three additional Isenhour houses built on Jesselin are just west of this grouping.

This house as originally built had a flat roof over the garage with this roof extending over the front entry.

1966
3465 LANNETTE LANE
LEXINGTON KENTUCKY

081 DAVIDGE

FRONT ELEVATION

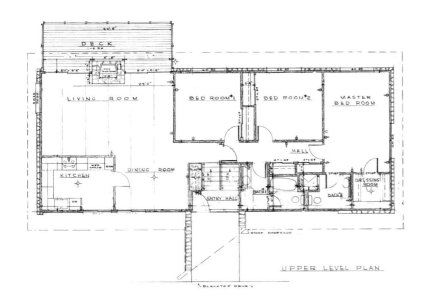

UPPER LEVEL PLAN

1966
1273 STANDISH WAY
LEXINGTON KENTUCKY

082 SMITH

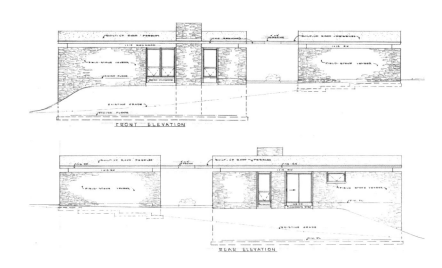

Richard Isenhour often specified limestone for his designs, as seen in the Smith house. The limestone used on so many of his houses is the same limestone that their very foundations rest on, a local and visually organic material.

According to Carolyn Murray-Wooley and Karl Raitz in their book *Rock Fences of the Bluegrass,* the Bluegrass itself rests on a limestone "dome," caused when inner geological forces lifted the rock beds of an ancient sea floor. Over millions of years, upper layers wore away, exposing layers of high-quality Oregon and Tyrone limestone that make excellent building materials.

This abundance of limestone tends to be a few feet below the surface, in contrast to fieldstone that was pulled up before plowing in the areas surrounding the inner Bluegrass. Stone exposed at outcroppings or near streambeds could be pried apart into slabs and broken into material for fences, foundations, or walls. In the early 1800s, Irish immigrant stonemasons fashioned limestone into rock fences and walls that are today a defining feature of Bluegrass horse farms.

Horizontal lines of laid-up masonry walls mimic the look of Kentucky River palisades, where plants grow out of rock fissures. Not only did Isenhour's stone houses utilize local materials, but also they replicated the local geography.

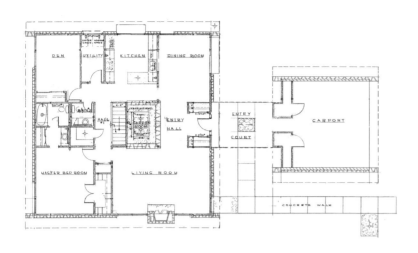

1967
837 CAHABA ROAD
LEXINGTON KENTUCKY

086 PARKS

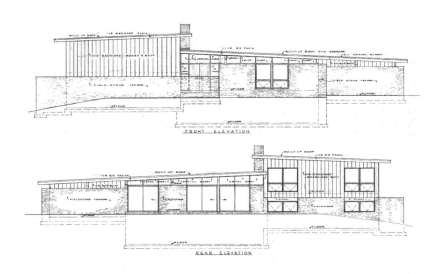

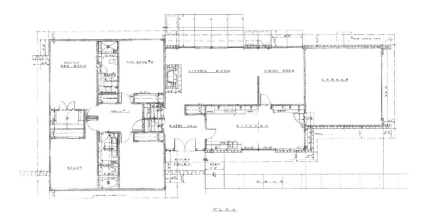

1967
2125 HART COURT
LEXINGTON KENTUCKY

087 HASBROUCK

FRONT ELEVATION

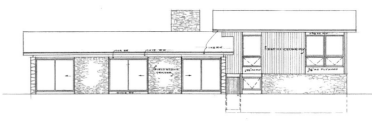

REAR ELEVATION

Richard Isenhour liked to design a house to fit the lay of the land, making the design work whenever possible using existing contours and working around existing trees. Many times his clients were drawn to the more difficult lots to build on, which made the completed house more interesting but made the design more of a challenge. The architect and his clients enjoyed the contrast with neighboring lots and houses where the earth was cut and filled to level so a stock house plan could be built.

Jan and Phyllis Hasbrouck moved to Lexington from New York where he was a member of the first class of interns at the new University of Kentucky College of Medicine.

They found a lot they liked that was covered with large trees and sloped down to the street below. The hill had been known as "Banana Holler," and it had been a favorite sledding location for local kids. Isenhour's final house design fit between the trees—except for one tree that would have been in the middle of the living room. Reluctantly, both architect and clients agreed that it had to be removed. These original trees still surround the house, including several elms and a hedge apple.

Visitors to the home have the feeling of being in a nature preserve rather than in the midst of a Lexington subdivision.

PLAN

1967
2129 HART COURT
LEXINGTON KENTUCKY

088 JONES

FRONT ELEVATION

REAR ELEVATION

Certainly the forms of Isenhour houses made them distinctive, but the color palette of the natural materials like stone and wood made them stand out from other houses in the neighborhood as well. Isenhour often brought these materials indoors: around the fireplace walls or at entry ways, where floors of stone lead to wood floors. Natural materials that are neutral and blend into interior walls and ceilings often provided the neutral palette preferred by architects.

Then out of this neutrality, a mid-century designer might pair earth tones with a brightly-colored wall or door accent, making them visually "pop." This mid-century use of color (on occasion as shockingly vivid as turquoise or orange) was a retort to drab colors from earlier decades.

In the Jones house, sunlight from the large window openings makes the colors even more vivid. The purple doors of the Hasbrouck house (see Job 087) and the interior blue pony wall of the Jones house show how Isenhour employed a sparing use of color to make an element stand out.

Original owners Joe and Margaret Jones were among many clients who commented on Isenhour's "punctiliousness," his strict attention to minute details.

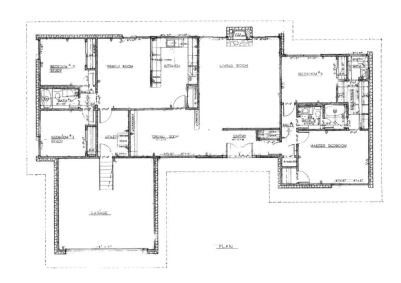

1967
3130 LAMAR DRIVE
LEXINGTON KENTUCKY

090 PROFFIT

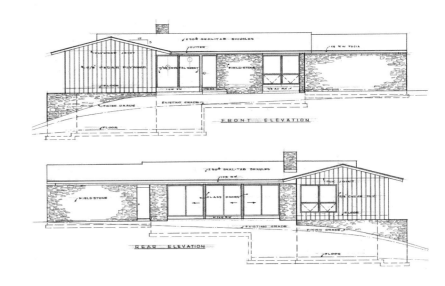

The Proffits became lifelong fans of the designs of Richard Isenhour. Dr. Proffit was the founding father of the University of Kentucky Dental School. The family was so comfortable with this home that after they left Lexington, they asked Isenhour to design two other houses for them: one in Gainesville, Florida, (Job 153) in 1973, and the other in Chapel Hill, North Carolina, (Job 165) in 1974. (See photo, page 157.)

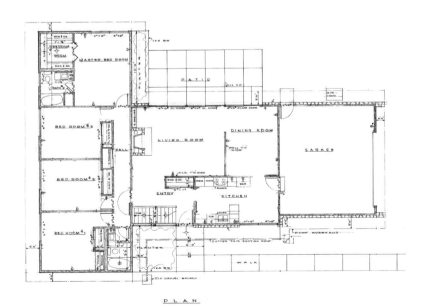

114

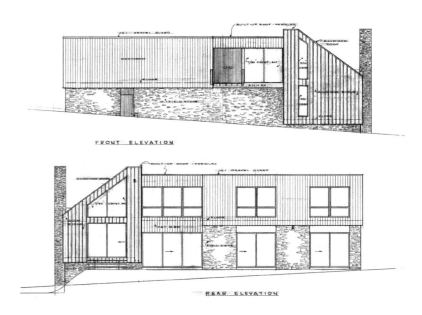

FRONT ELEVATION

REAR ELEVATION

1967
2017 LAKESIDE DRIVE
LEXINGTON KENTUCKY

091 GETTES

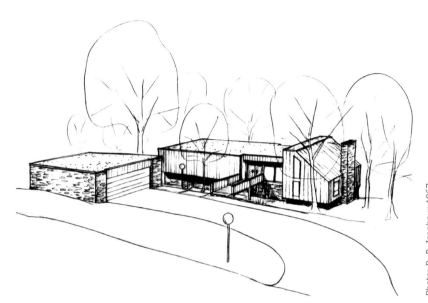

117

1968
2538 WESTMORLAND COURT
LEXINGTON KENTUCKY

095 FARABEE

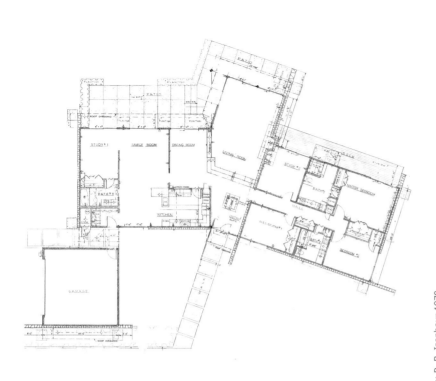

Photo: R. B. Isenhour 1970

Photo: R. B. Isenhour 1970

Photo: R. B. Isenhour 1970

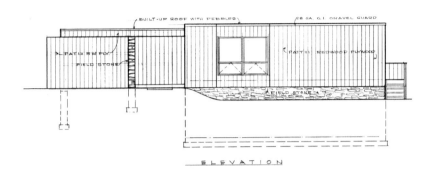

ELEVATION

1968
3367 SUTHERLAND DRIVE
LEXINGTON KENTUCKY

097 SMITH

Even after more than a decade of exposure to Richard Isenhour's designs, Lexington lending institutions were not always convinced about the lasting value of these new houses. As seen in the 1968 letter printed below, a Lexington savings and loan declined to fund "contemporary style homes because they are usually custom designed for a limited market."

The Smith house originally featured a flat roof with a cantilevered roof covering the carport. The rendering shows the house when built. The back is two stories, overlooking the creek below. The carport roof was designed to cantilever over the masonry wall some 12 feet without support.

November 21, 1968

Mr. Stanford Lee Smith
2443 Reims Road
Lexington, Kentucky   40504

Dear Mr. Smith:

We have reviewed your application for a mortgage loan commitment and regret that we will be unable to loan $25,200.00 on this property. Under our lending rules, we have difficulty in making the maximum loan on contemporary style homes because they are usually custom designed for a limited market.

I am returning to you our check for $25.00 which is a refund of your application fee and regret that we can not be of service to you at this time.

Yours very truly,

W. L. Woodward
Executive Vice President

WLW:bk

CC: R. B. Isenhour

1968
2049 LAKESIDE DRIVE
LEXINGTON KENTUCKY

099 HOLLINGSWORTH

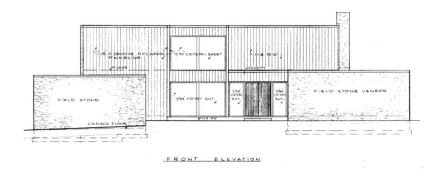

1969
955 EDGEWATER DRIVE
LEXINGTON KENTUCKY

130 KANNER

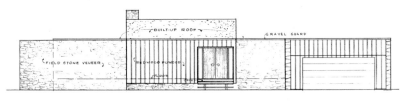

FRONT ELEVATION

1971
2025 LAKESIDE DRIVE
LEXINGTON KENTUCKY

144 ALLEN

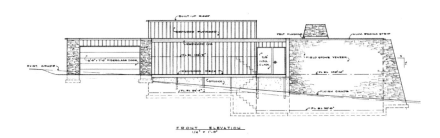

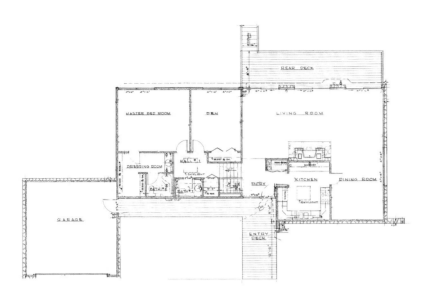

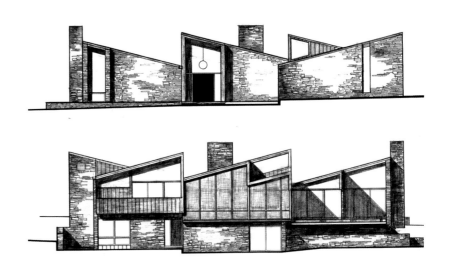

1972
2064 BRIDGEPORT DRIVE
LEXINGTON KENTUCKY

147 ISENHOUR

Just as the Isenhour house at 310 Blueberry Lane 16 years earlier had been an opportunity to put everything he was thinking about into one project, so the second Isenhour house on Bridgeport Drive was a design-idea occasion once again.

While Richard Isenhour worked on a house across the reservoir, he swam over and staked out the lot he would build on in the yet-to-be-finished subdivision on former water company property. Isenhour created and worked out many of the construction details in the field rather than on the drawing board. He seemed to be free to experiment with design elements and details here that may have been too bold on houses he built for clients. He lived for the next 34 years in this house, and it is the house most people in Lexington associate with his name.

The rear wall of the Isenhour house on Bridgeport, except for part of the master bath, is 100 percent glass. If his wife Lenora had agreed, it probably would have been glass too. A butt-glass corner in the dining space extends this glass wall around a corner without a mullion. From anywhere in the open living, dining, and kitchen areas, there is an unobstructed view of the backyard and lake. This is the ultimate in blurring the boundary of indoor and outdoor, and he loved it every day he lived there.

1972
491 SEELEY DRIVE
LEXINGTON KENTUCKY

148 KIELAR

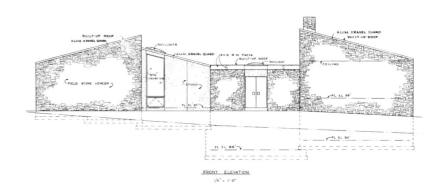

"Isenhour was here today and he tore out a wall." More than one original client has memories of Richard Isenhour's obsession with being a perfectionist. It was not unusual for him to check on a completed day's work, only to return to the truck for a sledge hammer to correct a quarter-inch misalignment or to remove something if he felt the quality was not up to standard. His carpenter crew knew to check things twice for dimension and being plumb. The drywall subcontractor knew to take the time to get walls smooth and in plane. Otherwise Isenhour would be there later with a flood lamp to make them get it right.

While plans were the guidelines for construction, the ways materials came together to make details work were sometimes in Isenhour's mind. It was not unusual for him to draw on plywood flooring or on a two-by-four block at the job site to show how a detail should be built—or sometimes how it should be rebuilt. Regardless, the detail would be built as Isenhour intended.

Richard and Carolyn Kielar came to Lexington from Ohio—he as a medical doctor and she as a designer and artist. They contracted with Isenhour to design their house and later a porch addition. They worked with him through the entire process and remember Isenhour correcting things that seemed fine to everyone else.

Photo: R. B. Isenhour 1974

134

1972
2105 BRIDGEPORT DRIVE
LEXINGTON KENTUCKY

150 HEARD

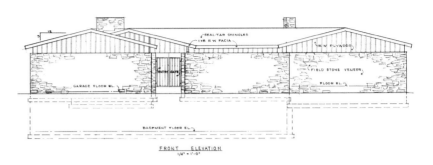

The Heard house is designed around a front courtyard, shielded from the street by a limestone wall. The metal gates, which were fabricated in 1976, define the courtyard as a private garden area while providing a view to the street.

Rod and Ann Heard came to Lexington from Texas and Oklahoma and were receptive to a southwest-style courtyard that would be a functional part of the house. They liked the idea of a courtyard that could be planted with a variety of shrubs and flowers.

The courtyard also brings light to the entry hall and other rooms through windows that open to the front court rather than the street. In turn, these rooms have views of the courtyard, reinforcing the mid-century modern notion of bringing the outside in.

An integral greenhouse also connects the house to plant areas year round. The family living area has windows that open to the greenhouse, which also serves as a passage from the garage to the kitchen.

The connections between indoor spaces and private outdoor surroundings add aesthetic value to the home.

1974
223 JESSELIN DRIVE
LEXINGTON KENTUCKY

158 CHAPMAN

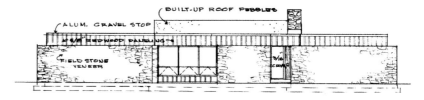

FRONT ELEVATION
1/8" = 1'-0"

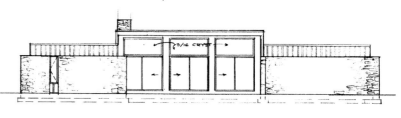

REAR ELEVATION
1/8" = 1'-0"

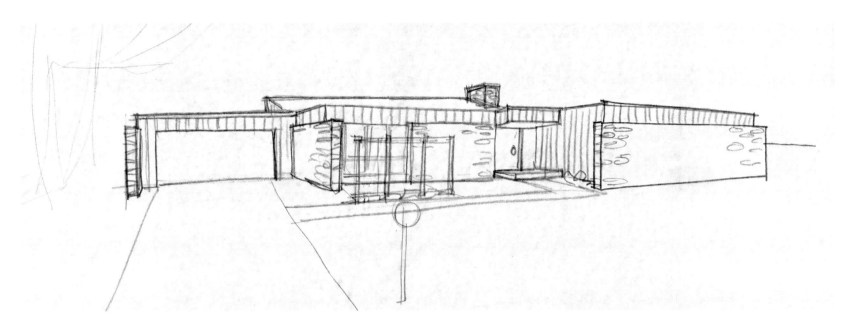

1974
2068 MANOR DRIVE
LEXINGTON KENTUCKY

161 RAY

FRONT ELEVATION

RIGHT SIDE ELEVATION

1974
2079 MANOR DRIVE
LEXINGTON KENTUCKY

168 KROMER

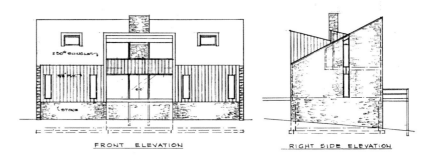

FRONT ELEVATION   RIGHT SIDE ELEVATION

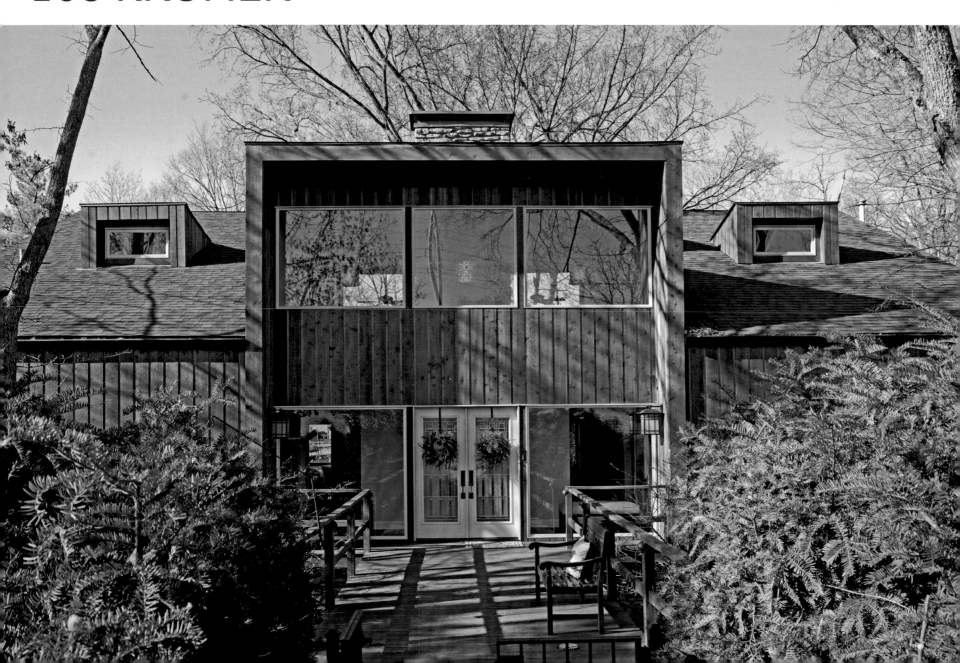

Photo: R. B. Isenhour 1976

Photo: R. B. Isenhour 1976

Photo: R. B. Isenhour 1976

1977
3617 GLOUCESTER DRIVE
LEXINGTON KENTUCKY

180 LORMAN

The Lorman house was not the only Isenhour design to reflect an Asian influence. Dr. Lorman had served in Korea with the medical corps. These owners had also traveled to India and Japan and had hosted Japanese exchange students.

In this residence, details which echo Japanese architecture appear to fit comfortably into a mid-century design. The Lorman residence includes a tea room with sliding shoji doors, whose translucent screens admitted a filtered light while providing privacy.

In fact, Japanese elements are present in the work of Frank Lloyd Wright, although Wright may have been more influenced by Japanese art than by Japanese architecture. Lexingtonian Clay Lancaster's 1963 book, *The Japanese Influence in America,* is often mentioned in connection with this debate. In characterizing Japanese residential architecture, Lancaster cites roofs that are low-pitched, covered with shingles or tiles. He also mentions that open galleries or verandas were common, which might be protected by overhanging eaves. Entrances were inconspicuous.

Regardless of the precise nature of the source, mid-century houses could share similarities with Asian design principles.

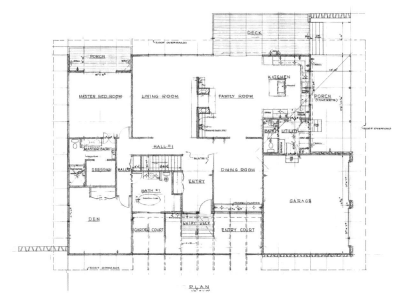

1978
3213 HOBCAW LANE
LEXINGTON KENTUCKY

189 WOLFF

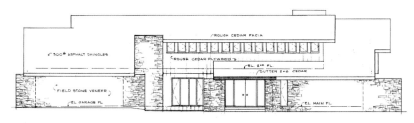

FRONT ELEVATION

When Fritz and Karin Wolff built their house in Lexington, they were desperate for a house "without columns." They felt the process of working with Richard Isenhour to build an open floor plan house on their wooded site was a wonderful experience.

Fritz Wolff grew up in Madison, Wisconsin, where he was immersed in the work of Frank Lloyd Wright. Wolff's grandfather, a German emigrant, was a skilled coppersmith, who started an architectural sheet-metal company with his son. The company did the metal roof work on many of the Frank Lloyd Wright houses in Wisconsin, including Taliesin. Wolff overheard conversations about copper finish treatment, as well as issues concerning water and payment.

As a child, Wolff played in Wright's Pew house, just down the street. He rode to Taliesin on his motorbike and talked with Wright before enrolling at the University of Wisconsin as an art studio major.

The Wolff house features horizontal lines and large overhangs over native limestone walls and wood. Limestone is laid with a textured look that results in protrusions of stone similar to those appearing on some of Wright's designs. Although the mid-century period would soon pass away, this house provides a clear indication of Wright's lasting influence over twentieth-century architecture.

Photo: R. B. Isenhour 1979

Photo: R. B. Isenhour 1979

R. B. ISENHOUR
BUILDING A MODERN LEXINGTON

Richard Isenhour 1973

Richard Isenhour began his career during a postwar period ripe with possibility and rich in new ideas. Early on, he benefitted from the experience of his father-in-law, the teachings of professors at Kentucky's new College of Architecture, the philosophies of housing expressed by Frank Lloyd Wright and the architects of the International Style, and the aesthetics of an informed clientele. He sampled and mastered a mid-century vocabulary: open floor plans, post-and-beam construction, walls of glass, connections to exterior spaces, and the convenience of modern materials. But in each of the just under 100 houses he designed and constructed, he put that vocabulary to the service of his own vision, a vision that while sometimes familiar remained nonetheless singular.

In a 1986 interview with the *Lexington Herald-Leader,* Isenhour said, "I tried one, then built another. Everyone—almost everyone—liked them. At least they sold." It would have been easy to find something that sold, then just keep repeating it.

But every house that Richard Isenhour designed was different. He took his clients' unique requirements and unique site conditions and created new solutions using elements and materials that he trusted. This collection of houses in chronological order allows us to see the similarities between houses, but also to see that each new house is something original.

The Introduction quotes from a 1947 letter that 22-year-old Richard Isenhour wrote to his future wife, Lenora Henry, questioning his career choice of chemical engineer: "The kind of job I'd like would be one that's creative and always changing, where I can see what I'm accomplishing. I'd like to work on things I can improve…" His body of work speaks for him. He found his calling.

The Isenhour houses were not just part of a national style that we identify as mid-century modern. Richard Isenhour worked on one house at a time and made a difference in one Kentucky town. His legacy is that he built a modern Lexington.

ISENHOUR DESIGNS NOT BUILT

068   *designed 1964*

084   *designed 1967*

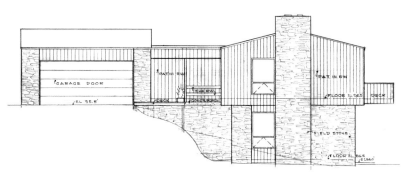

098   *designed 1969*

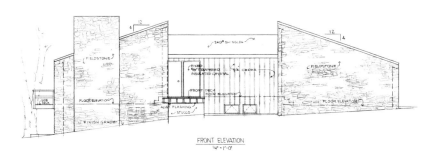

199   *designed 1978*

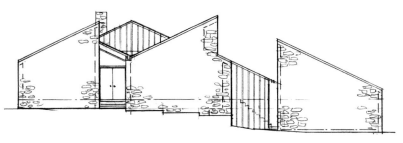

220   *designed 1983*

OTHER ISENHOUR DESIGNS

Photo: R. B. Isenhour 1974

151 Climate Control Office, 272 Big Run Road, Lexington, Kentucky 1973

055 LESTER 318, Jesselin Drive, Lexington, Kentucky 1961

089 MAYNARD, 292 Hightower Road, Lexington, Kentucky 1968

138 RICHARDSON, 1289 Maywood Park, Lexington, Kentucky 1970

165 PROFFIT, Chapel Hill, North Carolina 1974

179 DICKSON, 3221 Pepperhill Road, Lexington, Kentucky 1975

192 BROOKS, 735 Lakeshore Drive, Lexington, KY 1978

195 WIELAND, 2043 Manor Drive, Lexington, Kentucky 1979

208 HAILPERIN, 517 Bayberry Bend, Lexington, Kentucky 1979

211 BURNETT, 3140 Warrenwood Wynd, Lexington, Kentucky 1980

158

213 STAHMANN, 2040 Manor Drive, Lexington, Kentucky 1980

239 DERDERIAN, 3501 Winding Drive, Lexington, Kentucky 1983

243 BRIXIUS, 2309 The Woods Lane, Lexington, Kentucky 1984

244 COOPER, 1152 Tanbark Road, Lexington, Kentucky 1984

252 BROCKOPP, 2365 The Woods Lane, Lexington, Kentucky 1986

Photo: R. B. Isenhour 1988

259 HEIM, 993 Rockbridge Road, Lexington, Kentucky 1988

Photo: R. B. Isenhour 1988

261 MOORE, 3504 Castlegate Court, Lexington, Kentucky 1988

ACKNOWLEDGEMENTS

Thanks to the many people who helped create this book, including the following:

Jan Isenhour for co-writing the text and for copy editing. Ben Isenhour, Mason Dyer, and Celia Dyer for review of text. Katherine Henry and Carly Schnur for design layout guidance. Carol Butler for publishing advice.

Graham Pohl for providing the Foreword. (A previous version appeared in 2003 in the *Chevy Chaser.*)

The many original and current owners of Richard Isenhour houses who contributed their stories with enthusiasm and graciously opened their homes to be photographed: Douglas & Alice Logsdon, John & Victoria Hiett, Ken & Mary Lou Jackson, Jeremy & Catherine Sylvester, Greg Luhan & April Pottorff, Michael Troutman, Steven & Beth White, Benjamin Baker, Tom & Elizabeth Fielder, Bonnie Meyer, Diane King, Thom Smith, Kathryn Brinegar, Brian & Jennifer Moore, Art & Dixie Gallaher, Ron Saykaly, William & Persis Elwood, George & Natalie Wilson, Bob Mastin, Larry Smith, Phyllis Hasbrouck, Joseph & Margaret Jones, Craig Cornwell & Sandra Hough, Donald & Sandra Challman, Leonard & Margaret Ruth, Richard & Carolyn Kielar, Rod & Ann Heard, Kathleen Imhoff, and G. Fritz Wolff.

The children of Richard and Lenora Isenhour: Linda Klarer, Paul Isenhour, and Mark Isenhour who have contributed family memories and archive photographs to this text.

This book is dedicated to

Richard B. Isenhour

Lenora H. Isenhour